Comment Currency

How to Use Comments to Build Authority,
Visibility, and Opportunity on LinkedIn

Wendy Shore

SoMM Media

ISBN: 979-8-9954202-9-3
Published by Somm Media

"Leave comments. This is a real superpower of LinkedIn."
— Dan Roth, *Editor in Chief, LinkedIn*

Praise for Comment Currency

"Most people treat LinkedIn comments as an afterthought. This book will change that. Wendy breaks down exactly how to turn comments into currency, relationships into revenue, and visibility into real opportunities. This is the playbook for professionals who understand that where and how you show up matters especially when you're building an unforgettable presence."
— Lorraine K. Lee, *LinkedIn Founding Editor, Keynote Speaker, and Bestselling Author of Unforgettable Presence*

"Wendy Shore doesn't teach 'engagement.' She teaches trust. Comment Currency is a human first playbook for building authority the right way, through contribution, context, and real conversation. In a feed full of noise, this book reminds you that the comment section is where reputations are built, relationships are formed, and opportunity becomes inevitable. If you care about being felt, not just seen, read this."
— Joshua B. Lee, Founder, StandOut Authority | Creator of YOUmanize™

"Wendy Shore has done something rare: she's turned a LinkedIn behaviour most people overlook into a genuine business development system. Comment Currency is sharp, practical, and grounded in how LinkedIn actually works today — not how people assume it does. As someone who tracks LinkedIn's algorithm shifts closely through my Content & Algorithm Playbook, I can confirm that Wendy's approach is fully aligned with where the platform is heading. What I appreciate most is that this isn't theory — it's a repeatable system built from real professional experience. If you're serious about building authority on LinkedIn without burning out on content creation, this book belongs on your desk."
— Richard van der Blom, *LinkedIn Strategist & Algorithm Expert*

"We all forgot that social media is supposed to be social. Everyone's out here broadcasting, creating, posting, fighting for attention that's harder to earn every single day. Wendy's whole point is you don't win by adding more noise. You win by joining the conversations people are already paying attention to. Comment Currency lays out how to do that on LinkedIn. A simple system. Fifteen minutes a day, a few intentional comments. She shows you how that builds more trust and creates more opportunity than most people's entire content strategy. Once you read it, you'll wonder why you weren't doing this the whole time. Wendy gets it. Read this book."
— Scott D. Clary, *Host of the Success Story Podcast | Founder, WWA*

"LinkedIn comments are one of the most powerful ways to position your leadership online. What I love about Comment Currency is that Wendy shares an actionable formula for comments: visibility plus credibility equals opportunity. This is a must-read because it confirms why comments are a critical component of a strong LinkedIn strategy."
— Judi Fox, LinkedIn Business Consultant

"Comment Currency is the LinkedIn book I didn't know I needed. Wendy cuts through the noise of endless 'post more content' advice and reveals something genuinely counterintuitive: the comment section is where real authority is built. As someone who lives and breathes social media strategy, I can tell you, this is not theory. It's a practical, psychology-backed system that changes how you show up on LinkedIn and how the right people find you. If you're a business owner who wants visibility without burning out on content creation, this is your playbook."
— Katie Brinkley, CEO, Next Step Social | Author of The Social Shift"

"There's a big difference between commenting for visibility and engaging with intention. What stands out to me in Comment Currency is the emphasis on thoughtful, genuine interaction that aligns with your business goals — without losing the human element. This book gives practical advice on strategically leveraging your network to maximize your time and results, without crossing the line into manipulative or gimmicky growth tactics."
— Stacy Eleczko, Keynote Speaker + Messaging Strategist

"Comments are where the magic happens. I've said this for as long as I've been active on LinkedIn. Yet too many people still shrug them off as a waste of time. What I appreciate about this book is that it takes all the guesswork out of it. It lays out not only how to create an effective commenting strategy on LinkedIn, but why it matters that you do so. If this doesn't convince you to take commenting more seriously, you may want to rethink what your goals are on LinkedIn."
— Melissa Beth Cohen, *Personal Branding and LinkedIn Strategist, Founder MBC Consulting Solutions*

"LinkedIn visibility is usually framed as a posting game. Comment Currency reframes commenting as a serious authority-building mechanism driven by psychology, attention dynamics, and real interaction patterns. Every page feels grounded in lived experience rather than platform folklore. Read it and you'll never read a comment thread the same way again."
— Adriana Tica, *Marketing Strategist, Trend Analyst & Founder, Strategic AF Newsletter*

"I remember when I first cracked the code on visibility. After years of building the Women Helping Women Entrepreneurs® community to over 1 million women across social media, I thought I understood how attention worked online. I was wrong. Visibility isn't about who posts the most. It's about who adds the most value in the moments that matter. Everyone screams the same advice: post more, be consistent, chase the algorithm. And yes, posting matters. But what Wendy shares in this book? It's the part almost nobody talks about. The quiet power move: The comment

section. Wendy explains this in a way that just makes sense. She doesn't glamorize fake engagement. She doesn't chase vanity metrics. She shows you how visibility compounds when you contribute instead of perform. That's a lesson I believe in deeply. Because real growth, the kind that leads to clients, collaborations, and opportunity, doesn't come from shouting louder. It comes from showing up smarter. If you are building a business, if your reputation matters to you, if you want to be known for substance, not noise, read this book. Wendy has turned what most people treat as an afterthought into a strategy for real authority.
— Christina Rowe, Founder, Women Helping Women Entrepreneurs® | 1 Million Members

"Wendy's unique approach to growth through commenting had me hanging on every word! I loved learning how simple it is to engage with potential clients while adding value in a fun way. If you're serious about gaining more brand traction without the stress, I highly recommend this book!"
— Andrew Weiss, *Chief Marketing Officer, Podfest Expo*

"Through her personal experiences, Wendy Shore has found a way to utilize the power that LinkedIn can provide. Comment Currency will offer you some skills and tips to educate and enlighten you on how to use LinkedIn to enrich your professional life."
— Howie Karpin, *Award-Winning Sports Media Journalist and Bestselling Author*

For my kids,
who I love to the moon and back, and who never
stopped cheering for me, even through all the long
hours and late nights.

For my parents,
who always supported me, even when they didn't
understand me.

For my sister,
who always had my back.

And for the friends who believed in me before I
believed in myself.
You know who you are.

Foreword I

Some people do not just build businesses. They build momentum, clarity, and confidence in the people around them.

That is Wendy Shore.

I have had the pleasure of knowing Wendy since September 2023, and over that time, I have seen her bring a rare combination of insight, action, and energy. We have shared stages several times as LinkedIn expert panelists in NYC & DFW, contributed user insights through LinkedIn NYC HQ invites, and presented together at The Own Your Spotlight Summit in Raleigh.

Across every interaction, Wendy has been exactly who she appears to be in this book: thoughtful, experienced, action-oriented, and genuinely committed to helping people move forward.

That last part matters.

Because there are plenty of people who know how to talk about business growth, visibility, and branding. Far fewer know how to make those ideas practical, sustainable, and useful for real people with real demands on their time. Wendy does.

Comment Currency stands out because it's built on lived experience, not on trends or borrowed expertise. Wendy draws on over 30 years of experience in business leadership and strategy. Her writing has no fluff, no empty motivation, and not a "look at me" formula disguised as advice. The book's insight comes from real work.

And what she has uncovered is both simple and powerful.

Many professionals believe LinkedIn success starts with posting more. More content. More frequency. More hustle. Wendy offers a smarter path. She shows that meaningful comments are not an afterthought. They are often where visibility begins, where trust gets built, and where opportunity quietly takes shape. This book makes the case that thoughtful engagement can build authority faster and more naturally than constantly producing content from scratch.

That insight feels especially relevant right now.

In a professional world saturated with content, audiences seek substance, relevance, credibility, and meaningful exchange, not just volume. Wendy recognizes and addresses this need, standing apart from those who teach attention-chasing and instead guiding readers to earn trust.

That is very much in line with who Wendy is.

She is a go-getter in the best sense of the phrase. She finds a way through when others feel overwhelmed. She keeps moving. She helps others keep moving, too. And she brings a positive energy that makes hard things feel possible. That spirit runs through this book.

Her recent TEDx talk title says it all: "It Wasn't the Plan." What If It's Better? That mindset is woven into these pages. Because sometimes the breakthrough does not come from pushing harder on the old playbook. Sometimes it comes from seeing the opportunity that was there all along, just overlooked. Comment Currency is about one of those overlooked opportunities, and Wendy is exactly the right person to bring it to light.

If you are a business owner, executive, entrepreneur, creator, or professional who knows you have real value to offer but wants a more strategic and human way to become more visible, this book will meet you where you are.

And it will move you forward.

I am honored to introduce Wendy Shore and this timely, practical, and generous book.

Kevin D. Turner
Managing Partner, TNT Brand Strategist LLC

Foreword II

If you are reading this, you have probably felt the crushing weight of what I like to call "Content Chaos." That relentless churn of trends, algorithms, and the pressure to constantly create more, only to feel like you are connecting less.

You have probably been told that the only way to win on social media is to post constantly, join engagement pods, and shout into the digital void hoping someone hears you.

Here is the truth, and it is something that Wendy (the amazing human who wrote this book) and I agree on down to our bones: chasing visibility for the sake of visibility will flood your pipeline with unqualified leads, drain your energy, and pull you further from the people you are actually meant to serve.

The secret to winning is not louder.

It is deeper. Showing up with intention. Engaging like you mean it.

Which brings me to Wendy Shore.

When Wendy and I first connected, I knew right away she was someone I wanted in my corner. We bonded over a shared belief that business does not have to rely on complicated funnels, sleazy sales tactics, or selling your soul to the algorithm gods. And... she's a great hugger too!

But Wendy did not just share that belief and move on. She built a framework to prove it, and in doing so she uncovered something about LinkedIn that most people completely miss: Posts showcase your expertise, but comments build your authority.

In Comment Currency, Wendy shows you how to step off the content creation hamster wheel and into a far more powerful position.

Instead of fighting for attention in your own empty room, you learn how to walk into someone else's packed room, where the attention already exists, and use what she calls "borrowed reach" to build your visibility, your credibility, and your pipeline.

Organically.

This is not a growth hacks book. It is not about vanity metrics. Wendy breaks down the psychology of what she calls the "micro-trust loop," how a thoughtful, strategic comment can move someone from noticing you, to recognizing you, to trusting you, to eventually becoming a paying client. She also gets into LinkedIn's latest algorithm shifts and why the platform is actually rewarding depth, context, and authenticity right now.

At The Prepared Performer, we live by the motto: "The more fun we have, the more money we make." We also believe your "weird" is your absolute superpower, because Weird Wins. DUH!

Wendy's approach gives you a place to bring that wonderfully weird version of yourself directly into the conversations that matter.

You do not have to be a loud, performative content machine.

You just have to show up, add value, and connect like a human being.

So grab your favorite beverage... Coffee or maybe a Buttery Chardonnay. Whatever gets you in the zone. Wendy is about to hand you the playbook to turn the simple act of commenting into your most powerful business asset.

Get ready to amplify your voice, build your authority, and have a whole lot more fun doing it.

Molly Mahoney
CEO & Founder, The Prepared Performer
Author of Ai-ify Your Business

Introduction

The Business You Build in the Comments Section

I almost gave up.

Not on LinkedIn entirely, but on the strategy everyone said would work: Post consistently. Share valuable content. Build your audience. I was doing all of it. Two, three, sometimes four posts a week with over 30 years of real, earned experience behind every word.

And I wasn't getting anywhere.

I had maybe 1,500 followers, and I wasn't growing as quickly as I had thought I would. Meanwhile, people with a fraction of my experience (bro marketers with manufactured credibility, "business coaches" who'd never run a business, executive coaches who just graduated college) were growing in leaps and bounds. Ten thousand followers. Twenty thousand. Their secret? Engagement pods. Coordinated likes and comments that gamed the algorithm.

LinkedIn wasn't rewarding this behavior intentionally, but

these groups had figured out how to exploit the system, and it was working.

Then something wonderfully strange happened. I was recognized as a LinkedIn Top Voice. With under 2,000 followers. That's almost unheard of. Most Top Voices had tens of thousands of followers, sometimes hundreds of thousands. But LinkedIn's editors saw something in what I was doing. They recognized the quality of my contributions, even if the vanity metrics didn't reflect it yet.

That badge signaled that I was doing well, but I'll admit, it also confused me. If I was doing well, why did it feel like I was losing? Why were people with generic content and fake engagement growing faster? Why was I stuck?

I considered playing "the engagement pod game". For a moment, I thought, maybe I need to join one. Maybe this is just how it works now.

I couldn't bring myself to do it. LinkedIn mattered too much to me. My reputation mattered too much. I'd spent decades building credibility the hard way... through real work, real clients, real results. I wasn't about to trade that for inflated numbers.

Still, the question nagged me: If quality matters, why does it feel like quantity is winning?

I felt that I was doing all this for nothing. Then I got a DM (Direct Message). Someone I'd never met told me that something I'd posted had helped them solve a real problem in their business.

It wasn't about the likes or the reach. It was about the impact. That one message reminded me why I was doing this in the first place. But I also knew something had to change. I couldn't keep grinding out posts and hoping for traction. I needed a different strategy.

Around that time, I'd been contributing to LinkedIn Collaborative Articles. These were AI-generated topics where LinkedIn invites people to fill in the gaps, add context, share what's missing. I loved it. It felt natural. Less pressure. I wasn't staring at a blank screen trying to create something from nothing. I was adding to a conversation that was already happening.

And people responded. My contributions got traction. It felt... right.

I enjoyed contributing. But then, like everything else, it got gamed.

People started chasing gold badges through Collaborative Articles. Contribute everywhere, comment on everything, chase the algorithmic reward. It became another system to exploit for metrics. The quality dropped. The authenticity disappeared.

So I stepped away from the collaborative articles, but I couldn't shake that feeling I had when contributing to those articles. That sense of adding value to an existing conversation instead of shouting into the void.

What if I could take that same approach and apply it to regular posts?

It was like a lightbulb went off. I started engaging in the comments. Not with generic "Great post! " replies, but with real insights. Context. Experience. Perspective. The same kind of thoughtful contributions I'd been making in Collaborative Articles; just on other people's content.

And something remarkable started to happen...

Those comments turned into conversations. Sometimes in the thread, sometimes in the DMs. Conversations turned into Zoom calls. Zoom calls turned into clients, collaborations, and opportunities I never would have found by posting alone.

And LinkedIn noticed too.

In 2024, they began tracking metrics on individual comments: impressions, likes, replies: the same data they'd always shown for posts.[1]
If commenting wasn't valuable, they wouldn't be measuring it.

I realized I'd been playing the wrong game. Everyone told me to focus on my content. Post consistently. Build my audience. Grow my reach.

But the real momentum wasn't coming from my posts. It was coming from showing up in other people's audiences with something valuable to say.

Posts showcase your expertise. Comments build your authority.

That realization changed everything. I stopped chasing the algorithm and started building relationships. I began developing what became the foundation for this book: a system for using the comment section to build authority, visibility, and opportunity on LinkedIn.

LinkedIn confirmed I was onto something.

In late 2024, they rolled out a major algorithm update called 360Brew, a system designed to reward context, relevance, and genuine engagement. The platform was fighting back against the very behaviors that had frustrated me: pod gaming, AI-generated slop, and superficial engagement.

360Brew changed the rules. It evaluates not just what you post, but how you engage. It looks for depth, context, and authenticity. It rewards people who add value to conversations, not just those who post the most or gather the most likes.

The people winning on LinkedIn today aren't the ones chasing virality. They're the ones showing up with purpose in the places where conversations are already happening.

And that's what this book is about.

---

1. LinkedIn rolled out analytics on individual comments showing impressions, likes, and replies in 2024 – 2025, as discussed by LinkedIn VP of Product Management Gyanda Sachdeva and other LinkedIn executives.

Who This Book is for

This book was written with business owners, founders, and service-based professionals in mind, who want to turn LinkedIn into a source of credibility, clients, and community.

But these strategies work far beyond entrepreneurship. They also work for executives in or leaving corporate, and job seekers who need a safer, lower-risk way to become visible for what they know before they make their next big move.

Whether you are a corporate leader strengthening your thought leadership, a job seeker looking to stand out, a realtor building local authority, a creative professional growing your visibility, **or simply tired of being the best-kept secret in your industry**, the same principles in this book apply.

You'll use the same Visibility Funnel, the same daily routine, and the same AICE™ framework to build authority, visibility, and opportunity.

For executives who plan to leave corporate, comments are the safest way to start building a public reputation before you announce anything.
You don't have to post about "launching a business."
You can simply show up in conversations about your existing expertise: leadership, operations, culture, strategy, innovation, AI, or your specific industry. Your goal is to become known for how you think, long before you change your title.

For job seekers, comments are how you show you're more than a résumé. Every thoughtful reply is a live sample of how you think, communicate, and collaborate. Hiring managers and recruiters read comment threads. When they consistently see you adding insight to the topics they care about, you immediately stand out from the stack of applications that all look the same.

For founders, entrepreneurs, solopreneurs, and small business owners, comments are how you compete and build authority without a big following and with limited time. Every thoughtful comment puts you in front of audiences you didn't have to build yourself. You borrow the reach of others while demonstrating exactly the kind of expertise that turns strangers into clients.
You don't need to post every day or go viral. You just need to show up consistently in the right conversations with something worth saying. That's how you build authority organically — one comment at a time.

Contents

PART I
THE VISIBILITY SHIFT

Chapter One

The Hidden Power of Comments

Sarah is a business coach. She posts three times a week—tips, frameworks, client stories. Each post gets 200-300 views. She averages about 400 profile views per week.

Mark is also a business coach. He posts three times a week too. But he also takes the time to leave insightful replies on other people's posts as part of his posting strategy. He gets 1,000-3,000+ profile views per week.

Same time investment.
Same number of posts.
5-7x the visibility.

If you want visibility on LinkedIn, you have two choices: you can fight for attention or you can earn it. Most people choose the first. They post, hope, and refresh. The few who choose the second know a secret. **Attention is given to those who give attention first.**

That's why comments outperform posts in reach, relevance, and reputation.

LinkedIn's own Editor in Chief Dan Roth confirmed it:

"Leave comments. This is a real superpower of LinkedIn. **You can get really far on LinkedIn by just leaving comments — people look at your comments, they see other things you posted, they look at your profile...**"[1]

When you comment strategically, you're not chasing the algorithm; you're partnering with it. And the results compound. Visibility becomes familiarity. Familiarity becomes trust. Trust becomes opportunity.

Suddenly, you're not just another professional in their feed. You're the person they think of when they need help, a referral, or an expert opinion.

Why Comments Travel Further

Posts rely on followers. Comments ride the network.

When you post, your content is shown primarily to your existing followers. If you have 1,500 connections, maybe 300–500 people see your post. If it performs well, LinkedIn might push it a bit wider — but you're still starting from your own audience.

When you comment on someone else's post, the math changes entirely.

Let's say you comment on a post by someone with 10,000 followers. That post already has 50 other engaged commenters, each with their own networks. Your comment is now visible to:

- The original poster's 10,000 followers
- The other commenters and their connections
- Anyone who engages with the post after you

Suddenly, you're in front of 20,000, 30,000, sometimes 50,000+ people—most of whom would never have seen your content otherwise.

But here's what makes this visibility so powerful: **it's contextually relevant.**

You're not interrupting someone's feed with a cold pitch or a random post. You're appearing in a conversation they're already interested in, alongside a topic they already care about. Your insight is framed by the discussion around it.

That context does two things:
1. It makes people more receptive to what you have to say
2. It positions you as someone who belongs in that conversation

This is borrowed reach at its best—organic, targeted, and trust-building all at once. When you comment, you step into someone else's audience—where attention already exists.

The Real Metric: Meaningful Interaction

Here's what most people get wrong: they think visibility is about being seen.

It's not. It's about being engaged with... and remembered.

A comment that gets 100 views but zero replies is less valuable than a comment that gets 20 views and sparks three responses. Because those three responses signal something important: this person said something worth discussing.

That's the real metric. Not impressions. Not likes. Conversation.

When your comment prompts replies, even just one or two, it creates a ripple effect. More people see the thread. More people engage. The post gets pushed to more feeds. And your name appears alongside a conversation that's growing, not fading.

This is why generic comments fail. "Great post!" or "Great insight!" don't add any value to the conversation. They don't invite response. They end the discussion.

But a question like, "Have you found this approach works differently with remote teams versus in-office?" invites response. It opens a door. It gives people something to engage with.

And here's what happens when you consistently spark those micro-conversations:

People start recognizing you as someone who deepens discussions, not just reacts to them. Your comments become something people look for. Eventually, those people click your profile, send you a message, or think of you when an opportunity arises.

You're not building a follower count. You're building a reputation as someone worth engaging with.

And that's infinitely more valuable.

Your Takeaway
Every comment is an introduction, an impression, and an opportunity. Treat it that way.

This is the shift that separates Sarah from Mark. Sarah treats comments as afterthoughts, quick reactions before moving on. Mark treats them as strategic touchpoints, moments to add value, spark conversation, and be remembered.

You don't need to comment on every post. You don't need to write essays in the comment section. You just need to shift your intention.

Instead of writing to be seen, write to be remembered.

Bring a perspective, not just a compliment. Ask a question that moves the topic forward. Add context that clarifies, reframes, or challenges an idea.

When you do this consistently—even just a few times a week, you're no longer one of thousands posting into the void. You're part of the conversation shaping your industry. You're visible in the places that matter. And you're building authority one thoughtful comment at a time.

That's the hidden power of comments.

In the next chapter, we'll look at exactly how this visibility compounds and why the comment section might be the most underused opportunity on LinkedIn.

1. Roth, Dan. "New Rules of Career Growth with LinkedIn's Dan Roth." YouTube, February 26, 2026. https://www.youtube.com/watch?v=oBXYER49TPM&t=251s

Chapter Two

The Visibility Funnel

Think of LinkedIn like a series of rooms at a conference. As we touched on in chapter one, when you post, you're speaking in YOUR room. The only people who hear you are the ones who have already chosen to follow you into that room. Maybe it's 500 people. Maybe it's 5,000. Maybe it's even 50,000. But it's always the same crowd: your existing network.

When you comment, you're walking into SOMEONE ELSE'S room where their audience is already gathered, already engaged, already listening. You're not starting from scratch. You're joining a conversation that's already happening, in front of people who are already paying attention.

That's the visibility funnel.

You don't post anything. You don't promote anything. You just join the right conversation with something worth saying.

It works like this: You show up in the comments where conversations are already happening. You add value. People notice. Some of them follow you back to YOUR room. They want to hear more of what you have to say. **Over time, borrowed visibility becomes owned authority.**

The visibility funnel isn't about chasing attention. It's about earning it. By showing up where attention already exists and adding something worth remembering, you earn your way into new networks one thoughtful comment at a time.

The Five Stages of the Visibility Funnel

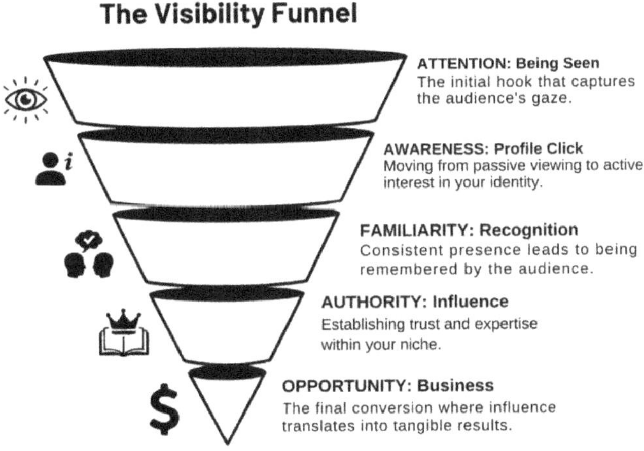

Stage 1: Attention

Comments put you in front of audiences you didn't have to build yourself. When you engage on someone else's post, you borrow their visibility. You step into a spotlight that already exists.

The author sees you. Their network sees you. Anyone scrolling through the conversation thread sees you. And for that moment, you have their attention.

Most people try to build visibility by posting more. More content. More consistency. More volume. And that works. Eventually. (And you absolutely need to do it as part of your strategy.) But it's slow. You're limited by your existing network and the algorithm's willingness to push your content beyond it.

Commenting flips the equation. Instead of waiting for people to find you, you show up where they already are. That's borrowed reach. It's visibility without the wait of building an audience from scratch.

The key here isn't to chase "big rooms." It's to show up in the right ones (where your ideal audience is already listening) and add something worth reading once you're there.

Stage 2: Awareness

Your comment catches someone's attention, and they click your profile. That's the spark of awareness.

This is why what you say matters. Every comment is a signal: a micro-impression of your expertise, perspective, or insight. It either earns attention or gets scrolled past.

When your comment earns that click, you have a three-five-second window. They land on your profile. They scan your headline. They glance at your banner. They might skim your recent posts.

In that moment, everything needs to align. Your profile should reinforce what your comment just promised: clarity about who you are, what you know, and why you're worth following.

If your comment said something insightful about client retention, but your profile talks about graphic design, you lose them.If your comment was thoughtful and strategic, but your headline is vague or generic — you lose them.

When the comment and profile tell the same story, it signals to the algorithm that you're sharing valuable expertise. That first impression (your name, your comment, your tone) creates curiosity. What they see when they click determines whether they keep scrolling or decide to follow.

Stage 3: Familiarity

The more someone sees you, the more they trust you, even if they've never interacted with you directly. It's a strange phenomenon. Psychologists call it the mere exposure effect.

You're no longer a stranger commenting on posts. You're that person who always has something smart to say about [your expertise]. You're on their mental list of people worth paying attention to.

This is where consistency matters more than followers. You could have 50,000 connections and still be invisible. Or you could have 2,000 and be unforgettable—because you show up in the right conversations, consistently. You don't need viral posts or massive reach. You just need to keep showing up in the right places with insights that add to the conversation, not just echo it.

Maybe they see you weigh in on a pricing strategy post on Monday. Then you're in a thread about client communication on Thursday. A week later, you're adding nuance to a discussion about AI for business growth. Each touchpoint builds on the last. You're not everywhere. But it seems like it, because you're consistently somewhere valuable.

Within weeks (and sometimes just days) people who've never met you start to feel like they know you. They anticipate your take on certain topics. They remember your phrasing. They recognize your tone.

That's not coincidence. It's pattern recognition. And pattern recognition is how authority starts to form.

Stage 4: Authority

Authority doesn't come from announcing that you're an expert. It comes from showing up and adding so much value that other people start to say it for you.

You're no longer just participating in conversations, you're influencing them. They reference your perspective in their own posts. They echo your phrasing, your frameworks, your way of thinking about the problem.

This is the authority stage, and you earned it...one contribution at a time.

Engage with insight, context, and confidence, and people start to associate your name with expertise. You become the go-to, the person others think of first when a topic in your field comes up. Not because you're the loudest voice, but because you've been the most consistently insightful one.

That's authority built organically.

And here's the beauty of it: this kind of authority is self-sustaining. Once people trust your perspective, you don't have to keep proving it. Every thoughtful comment you add simply reinforces what they already believe about you.

Authority isn't a title. It's a reputation. And your reputation is built in the comments section—one conversation at a time.

Stage 5: Opportunity

Opportunities arise where visibility and authority meet. It's the moment when being seen turns into being sought after. You never know which comment will spark it. Sometimes it's a quick observation that resonates. Sometimes it's a thoughtful response that makes someone think differently. But at some point, it happens.

You get a DM from someone you've never met:
"I've been following your comments for a few months now. I love how you think about [topic]. We're looking for someone to help with [project]. Are you taking on new clients?"

or "I loved what you said on somebody's post. I feel your services are exactly what I need right now. Can we talk?"

You get an email:
"Would you be interested in speaking at our conference? We've seen your insights on LinkedIn and think our audience would benefit from your perspective."

Or it's a referral:
"I don't know them personally, but I've seen them comment on posts about [your expertise] for months. They clearly know their stuff. You should reach out."

This is Stage 5. Where visibility, familiarity, and authority converge into actual business.

These opportunities don't feel random. They feel inevitable. Because they are.

Every comment is a demonstration. Every interaction is a chance to show how you think, communicate, and contribute. The more often you do it with intention, the more the right people start to notice... and remember. Because you've been building trust in public, one comment at a time, long before anyone reached out.

The person who DMs you isn't taking a risk. They've already watched you demonstrate your expertise. They're not wondering if you know your stuff, they already believe you do. They're just finally ready to work with you.

It's what makes people refer you to colleagues even though they've never hired you themselves. Recommend you for speaking gigs even though you've never met. Trust you enough to make an introduction before ever working together.

That's the business you build in the comments section.

Not through cold outreach or aggressive pitching. Through consistent, valuable presence that makes people want to work with you before you ever ask.

"Commenting gets you noticed.
Posting builds credibility.
Together, they turn attention into opportunity."

THE "EVERYONE READING" RULE

Unlike most other platforms where comments are an afterthought, LinkedIn users actually read comment threads, especially when a post gains traction. That's because the conversation in the comments often adds more value than the post itself.

People share experiences, ask thoughtful questions, and offer perspectives that deepen the discussion.

It seems as if LinkedIn treats comments as core content, while platforms like Facebook and Instagram historically treat them as secondary. This creates a unique opportunity: everyone reading the comments is already in learning mode. They're engaged. They're curious. They're evaluating what's being said—and who's saying it.

When you comment, you're not just visible. You're being assessed. People are subconsciously asking themselves:

• Does this person know what they're talking about?

• Is this insight valuable?

• Should I follow them?

That's why we emphasize that generic comments like "Great post!" waste the opportunity. You had everyone's attention for a split second—and gave them nothing.

The "Everyone Reading" Rule is simple: Write every comment as if the person you most want to work with is watching. Because they might be.

Chapter Three

The Psychology of Engagement

S omeone you've never met sends you a connection request. You click their profile. It's polished. Nice headline, professional photo, well-written summary. You accept the request and immediately forget about them.

Another person you've never met appears in your feed. Not in your inbox, but in a comment thread you're reading. They add a perspective you hadn't considered. The next week, you see them again in a different thread. Then again. You don't send them a connection request, but you just start noticing them. Perhaps you start following them.

Six months later, when someone asks if you know a good [their expertise], their name is the first one that comes to mind.

That's the psychology of engagement.

Every time you comment, you're revealing something most content can't: who you are when you're not performing.

You're showing how you think, communicate, and engage with ideas in real time.

Why Interaction Builds Trust Faster Than Content

There's a difference between telling people you're good at what you do and showing them.

Your LinkedIn profile tells. Your posts tell. Even your recommendations and testimonials tell. They're static. Curated. Designed to present the best version of you.

Comments show.

When you comment, you're demonstrating how you think in real time. You're not crafting the perfect message or workshopping your words for days. You're responding to someone else's idea, adding context, offering a perspective, maybe even disagreeing thoughtfully.

That's more convincing than any 'About section' could ever be.

Because people don't just want to know what you know. They want to see how you think. How you communicate under pressure. How you handle disagreement. Whether you're generous with your insights or protective of your expertise.

Comments reveal all of that.

When you comment, you're not just visible, you're visible in context. You're not saying "I'm great at X." You're proving it by adding value to a conversation about X. The context does the credibility work for you.

The Five Second Judgement

(Psychologists call it "thin slicing")

When someone reads your comment, their brain is scanning for cues of credibility, warmth, and authority... all within seconds. It's the ability to form lasting impressions from small bits of information.

A thoughtful comment demonstrates three things at once:

1. **Competence** — You know your subject.

2. **Character** — You contribute with respect and clarity.

3. **Care** — You're paying attention to the conversation, not just promoting yourself.

Posts can tell people you're smart. Comments prove it. That's why a single thoughtful comment can build more trust than a perfectly written profile summary. Because trust isn't built through claims. It's built through proof.

The Mirror Effect: Why Relatability Compounds Trust

When you share a story or experience in a comment — something that happened to you, a mistake you made, a lesson you learned the hard way — something powerful happens in the reader's mind.

They think: "That happened to me too."
Or: "I've been there."
Or: "This person gets it."

Expertise makes people respect you. Relatability makes people trust you.

People connect fastest with people who sound like them or who say what they were already thinking but hadn't yet articulated. When someone sees their own experience reflected in yours, it creates an instant bond. Not just recognition, but connection. This is the mirror effect.

This is different from being insightful or strategic. Those qualities make you look smart. The mirror effect makes you feel human. And humans trust humans. Which is becoming even more important in the age of AI.

The Difference Between Authority and Relatability

You can establish authority by saying: "Based on my 15 years of experience, the best approach is..."

That's credible. It positions you as an expert.

But you create relatability by saying: "We tried this approach with a client last year and it completely backfired. Turned out we were solving the wrong problem..."
That's real. It positions you as someone who's been in the trenches.

Authority says: I know the answer. Relatability says: I've lived the question.

Both matter, but on LinkedIn, where everyone is trying to look polished and perfect, relatability stands out.

How to Use the Mirror Effect in Comments

You don't need to overshare or turn every comment into a therapy session. But when you can add a brief, relevant story or experience that mirrors what others might be going through, do it.

Instead of: "Great point about client communication."
Try: "This reminds me of a project where we lost a client because we assumed they understood our process. Turns out, we never actually explained it. Now we over-communicate—and it's saved us more than once."
Or: "We started doing this last year and honestly, the biggest benefit wasn't what we expected. Yes, communication improved. But we also uncovered three upsell opportunities we would've missed entirely. It changed how we think about client onboarding."

The first requires no thought and suggests you barely read the post. The second and third are memorable and show others your experience.

When people see themselves in your experience, trust accelerates. They're not just learning from you, they're recognizing that you understand their world. And that recognition is the foundation of every strong professional relationship.

The Micro-Trust Loop

People don't buy from the most visible person. They buy from the most trusted one.

Trust doesn't happen all at once. It accumulates. Every time someone sees you add value to a conversation, whether they engage with you directly or just observe from the sidelines—you make a small deposit into what we'll call the micro-trust loop. And it doesn't happen through automation or outreach. It happens through genuine contribution. Here's how it works:

1. You comment thoughtfully.
Someone sees it. They might not react. They might not even remember your name yet. But their brain registers: "That was useful."

2. You show up again.
A week later, they see you in another thread. Same quality. Same generosity. Another useful contribution. Their brain registers: "I've seen this person before. They're consistent."

3. Repetition builds recognition.
The third, fourth, fifth time they encounter you, something shifts. You're no longer random. You're familiar. And familiarity feels like trust, even if they've never interacted with you directly.

4. Trust compounds.
Eventually, they don't just recognize you. They seek you

out. They look for your comments. Over time, repeated exposure in the right context builds trust. They click your profile. They follow you. And when they need what you offer, you're the first person they think of. That's the micro loop in motion: visibility that builds on itself, powered by consistent contribution.

Value → Recognition → Familiarity → Trust → Opportunity.

And it all starts with one comment.

Why Frequency Matters More Than Intensity

Most people think trust is built through big moments—viral posts, major wins, impressive credentials.

But the micro-trust loop works differently. It's not about intensity. It's about frequency.

> Would you trust someone more if they:
>
> • Posted one polished, in-depth article once a month?
> • Or left three thoughtful, insightful comments every week?
>
> The second option wins. **Because trust is built through repeated exposure, not occasional brilliance.**

This is why consistency beats perfection on LinkedIn. You don't need to have the best comment every time. You just need to show up reliably, in the right conversations, with something worth saying.

Think of it like planting a garden. You don't plant seeds, water once, then come back a month later expecting vegetables. You water it consistently. You nurture it. Trust grows the same way.

The Compounding Effect

Here's what makes the micro-trust loop so powerful: each deposit builds on the last.

The first time someone sees you comment, you're a stranger. The second time, you're vaguely familiar. The third time, they start to recognize you. By the fifth or sixth time, they feel like they know you.

That's the compounding effect.

Individually, comments don't seem like much. But together, they create momentum that even a viral post can't replicate.

This is why people who comment consistently for six months often see exponential results. Not because any one comment went viral, but because the trust deposits compounded into authority over time.

One comment earns attention. Repetition earns trust. Consistency earns authority.

The Reciprocity Effect: From Contribution to Connection

There's a powerful psychological principle at work when you comment thoughtfully on LinkedIn: reciprocity.

When you give something of value: an insight, a perspective, a story that helps someone think differently, people feel a natural pull to give something back.

It's not transactional. It's human.

Psychologists have studied this for decades. When someone does something helpful for us, we feel compelled to return the favor. It's wired into how we build relationships and maintain social bonds.

On LinkedIn, reciprocity shows up in subtle but powerful ways:

• You leave a thoughtful comment on somcone's post. They click your profile, read your content, and follow you back.

• You add value to a thread. The original poster notices and engages with your next post.

• You contribute consistently in someone's comment section. Six months later, they refer a client to you, even though you never asked.

You're not doing this to "get" something. But when you give first—publicly, generously, consistently—people notice. And they want to reciprocate.

Why This Matters for Building Your Business

Too many people approach LinkedIn (and relationships off the platform) with a "take first" mentality:

- They connect with someone, then immediately pitch their services (also known on LinkedIn as the "pitch-slap")

- Comment on somebody's post to promote their own content or drop their own link.

- DM strangers asking for introductions or referrals

That's not reciprocity. It's selfish and people can feel it.

Strategic commenting flips the script. You give first. You add value without asking for anything in return. You show up generously, repeatedly, in conversations that matter to your audience. And over time, that generosity compounds into something tangible: The followers who engage with your content

- The connection requests from people who want to know you better

- The DMs from potential clients who've been watching you for months

- The referrals from people who've never worked with you but trust you anyway

You can't force reciprocity. But you can create the conditions for it.

When you comment with genuine intention to add value;not to be seen, not to promote yourself, but to contribute something useful, reciprocity follows naturally.

From Reciprocity to Relationship

LinkedIn creates relationships. And relationships are the real algorithm. They beat every hack, every trend, every gaming tactic. Every time.

When someone sees you show up thoughtfully in their world (commenting on their posts, adding to their ideas, engaging with their community), they start to see you as an ally, not a stranger.

That shift changes everything.

Suddenly, they're not evaluating you as someone trying to sell something. Instead, they're thinking of you as someone who "gets it" or someone they should know better. And when that happens, the relationship becomes real. Not performative. Not transactional. Real.

This is why the best opportunities on LinkedIn don't come from pitching. They come from contributing. From showing up generously, over time, in ways that help others succeed.

Reciprocity isn't a tactic. It's the natural result of giving value without keeping score.

Visibility Formula
Why Visibility + Credibility = Opportunity.

> *Visibility alone = "I've heard of you."*
> *Credibility alone = "I trust you, but I didn't think of you."*
> *Visibility + Credibility = "You're exactly who I need."*

You can be seen by thousands of people and still get no business. Plenty of people have large followings and empty inboxes. They're visible, but they're not trusted.

You can be the best in your field, trusted by everyone who knows you, but if only 50 people know you exist, your impact is limited. You're credible, but not discoverable.

The magic happens at the intersection.

When you're both visible AND credible, opportunity becomes inevitable. Because people don't just see you; they trust you. And when they need what you offer, you're the obvious choice.

Why Most Strategies Give You One or the Other, But Not Both

Traditional networking gives you credibility within a small circle. People know you, trust you, refer you. But it doesn't scale. You're limited by the size of your network and the strength of your relationships.

Content marketing gives you visibility and builds trust with your existing audience. Post consistently, and people will see you. Over time, trust can build. But you're limited by your audience size and the algorithm's willingness to push your content beyond your existing connections.

Paid advertising gives you reach but not trust. When people see your ad, they might click on it. But they're evaluating you as a stranger, not as someone they already believe in.

Strategic commenting gives you both. Every time you comment thoughtfully:

• You're visible to new audiences (borrowed reach)

• You're demonstrating expertise in context (building credibility)

• You're showing up repeatedly in the right conversations (compounding trust)

That combination is rare. And powerful.

That's why commenting works. It's not just a visibility strategy. It's not just a credibility strategy. It's both. ***And that's what creates opportunity.***

PART II
STRATEGIC COMMENTING

***

You've been commenting out of habit.
Scrolling. Reacting. Dropping a thoughtful comment here
and there on whatever catches your eye.
And nothing's happening.
That ends now.
You're going to stop engaging out of habit
and start engaging with intent.

Chapter Four

Set Your Intentions

You don't need to comment more. You need to comment smarter.

You could spend an hour commenting on LinkedIn every day and get absolutely nowhere. Or you could spend 20 minutes with clear intention and build real momentum toward the business you want.

The difference? Knowing why you're commenting before you start typing.

Most people treat LinkedIn like a slot machine. They scroll, they comment on whatever catches their eye, they hope something good happens. But hope isn't a strategy. And random engagement doesn't build authority.

Strategic commenting starts with one simple question: What am I trying to accomplish with this comment?

There are three reasons to comment on LinkedIn:
1. Visibility – Get seen by new audiences
2. Credibility – Demonstrate your expertise
3. Connection – Build relationships with specific people

Every comment you write should serve at least one of these purposes. Ideally, all three.

Let's break down each one.

Commenting for Visibility

When you comment for visibility, you're accessing someone else's audience.

Every comment you write can potentially appear in the feed of:

- People who follow YOU

- People who follow the ORIGINAL POSTER

- People who have already commented on that post

- People in LinkedIn's network who engage with similar content

That's potentially thousands of people you don't already know who could see your name, your face, and your insights.

This is borrowed reach at scale.

If you comment on a post from someone with 10,000 followers, you potentially just showed up in front of 10,000 people you couldn't have reached on your own. And you didn't have to spend a dime on ads or hours creating content to get there.

But here's where most people screw this up: They comment on posts from people with massive followings and zero relevance to their business.

Visibility without relevance is just noise.

If you're a business coach, commenting on a viral meme about cats might get you impressions. But those impressions don't convert into opportunities because the people seeing your comment aren't your ideal clients.

Visibility done right:

- Comment on posts from people whose audiences overlap with your ideal client profile

- Look for posts with high engagement already (LinkedIn rewards momentum)

- Choose posts where your expertise is relevant to the conversation - Prioritize posts from people in your industry or adjacent industries

Example:

Let's say you're a LinkedIn strategist for B2B founders. You see two posts in your feed:

Post A: A general motivational quote about entrepreneurship from someone with 50,000 followers.

Post B: A founder with 5,000 followers asking, "What's your biggest LinkedIn challenge right now?"

Post A will get you more eyeballs. Post B will get you better eyeballs.

The founder's post is a magnet for your exact audience—people actively struggling with LinkedIn who are already engaged enough to comment. That's the visibility you want.

Commenting for Credibility

Credibility isn't about having the most followers. I know plenty of people with massive followings that I wouldn't trust to tie my shoelace. It's about being known for something specific and having the real experience to back it up.

When you consistently comment with insight in a particular area, people start associating you with that expertise. They might not remember every comment you make, but they'll remember the pattern: "This person always knows what they're talking about when it comes to [your thing]."

This is how you build authority without creating content.

Credibility done right:

- Comment on topics where you have real expertise

- Add depth, not just agreement (we'll cover this in the next chapter)

- Be consistent (show up regularly in valuable conversations) - Use positioning language ("In my experience..." or "I've seen this work when...")

Here's the key distinction most people miss:

Your comments can be broad. Your posts should be focused.

If you're a brand strategist, you can comment on posts about social media algorithms, pricing strategy, and brand positioning. All three will get you noticed and bring eyeballs to your profile.

But when people click through to see who you are? Your posts should be laser-focused on brand positioning. That's what establishes you as THE person who understands positioning.

Comments get you visibility across topics. Posts prove your expertise in one.

Example:

You comment on a pricing strategy post with a smart observation about how pricing communicates brand value. Someone clicks your profile. They see post after post about brand positioning; frameworks, case studies, insights.

The comment got their attention. The posts earned their trust.

That's how you build credibility that converts.

Commenting for Connection

Sometimes, you're not commenting for a big audience. You're commenting to build a relationship with one specific person. Maybe it's a potential client. Maybe it's someone whose work you admire. Maybe it's a strategic partner who could open doors for you.

When you comment on their posts consistently — not every single time, but regularly — you become familiar to them. They start recognizing your name. They see you showing up with insights, not just flattery.

And when you eventually send them a DM or a connection request, you're not a stranger. You're someone who's already been part of their world.

Connection done right:

- Identify 5-10 people you want to build relationships with
- Engage on their posts consistently (not obsessively)
- Add value in your comments, don't just say "Great post!"
- Be genuine—people can smell fake engagement a mile away

This is the long game. You're not going to comment once and land a client. But over time, consistent, thoughtful engagement builds familiarity, and familiarity builds trust.

Example:

You want to work with a specific company. You identify three executives at that company who are active on LinkedIn.

Instead of cold-pitching them, you spend three months engaging on their posts. Not every post, just the ones where you have something meaningful to add.

After three months, they recognize your name. When you reach out with a message, they're already warmed up. You're not some random person in their inbox. You're someone who's been part of their conversations.

Choosing Where to Spend Your Energy

You don't have time to comment everywhere. If you try to be visible, credible, AND build connections with everyone, you'll burn out and accomplish nothing.

You need to be selective.

Start by asking yourself:

What's my primary goal right now?

- If you need visibility, prioritize posts with large, relevant audiences

- If you need credibility, prioritize posts where you can demonstrate expertise

- If you need connections, prioritize posts from specific people you want relationships with

Who do I want to reach?

- Ideal clients

- Referral partners

- Industry influencers

- Adjacent professionals who serve the same audience

Where are those people already engaging?

- Look for posts with high comment activity (that's where conversations happen)

- Pay attention to who's commenting (are they your

people?)

- Notice patterns (certain topics, certain posters, certain times of day)

Then create a commenting strategy around those insights.

A simple system:

1. Identify 10-15 people whose audiences align with your business goals

2. Turn on post notifications for 3-5 of them (so you can comment early)

3. Set a timer for 20 minutes a day and focus ONLY on those posts

4. Rotate your focus every month or two to keep expanding your network

   Why rotate? You rotate to keep reaching fresh people, expanding your community, and building new relationships. Your goal is network growth, not just engagement depth with the same 15 people forever.

The Connection Level Strategy:

You could do this with your 1st-degree connections — people you're already connected to. And you should engage with them.

But here's where the real leverage is: Focus on 2nd-degree connections.

When you comment on a 2nd-degree connection's post, you're showing up in front of their network: people who don't know you yet but are one degree away. When those people see your comment and click your profile, they're 3rd-degree connections. That's brand new territory. That's how you expand your reach exponentially.

Example:

You're connected to Sarah (1st-degree). Sarah is connected to Marcus (your 2nd-degree). Marcus has 5,000 followers, many of whom are your ideal clients (your 3rd-degree connections).

If you comment thoughtfully on Marcus's posts:
- Marcus sees you (2nd-degree → potential 1st-degree connection)
- His 5,000 followers see you (3rd-degree → potential 2nd-degree connections)

You just got in front of thousands of people you couldn't have reached otherwise.

So while you should absolutely engage with your 1st-degree connections, **prioritize your 2nd-degree connections.** That's where the network expansion happens.

That is commenting smarter.

Once you've identified your 15 people, you need a way to actually find their content without scrolling aimlessly through your feed. In Part III, I'll show you two simple systems for organizing your list so you can access their posts in seconds — no searching, no algorithm guessing. For now, just focus on identifying who these 15 people should be.

Training Your Feed

Here's something most people don't realize: LinkedIn is watching where you engage.

Every time you comment on a post, you're telling the algorithm, "I want to see more content like this."

Comment on a lot of motivational quotes? LinkedIn will show you more motivational quotes.

Comment on a lot of tactical business strategy posts? LinkedIn will show you more of those.

Your feed is trainable. And if you're intentional about where you comment, you can curate a feed that actually serves your business.

How to train your feed:

1. Engage consistently on posts from people in your target industry

2. Ignore (don't engage with) content that's off-brand for you

3. Use the "Not interested" option on posts that dilute your feed

4. Comment on posts that reflect the expertise you want to be known for

Over time, your feed becomes a goldmine of opportunity. Full of posts from your ideal clients, referral partners, and industry leaders — All because you were strategic about where you showed up.

The 80/20 Rule

Here's where most people get LinkedIn backwards: They spend 80% of their time creating content and 20% engaging with others.

Flip it.

Spend 80% of your time commenting on other people's content. Spend 20% creating your own posts.

This feels counterintuitive. You've been told you need to post consistently to build a brand. and that's true; your posts do matter.

When you comment, you're doing three things simultaneously:
1. Getting in front of new audiences (visibility)
2. Demonstrating your expertise in real-time (credibility)
3. Building relationships with the people who matter (connection) Your posts can't do all three at once.

Here's what the 80/20 split looks like in practice:

If you have 30 minutes a day for LinkedIn:

- Spend 24 minutes commenting on other people's posts (including responding to comments on your own posts)

- Spend 6 minutes creating your own content

If you have an hour a day:

- Spend 48 minutes engaging strategically

- Spend 12 minutes writing posts

This isn't a hard rule. Some weeks you'll create more. Some weeks you'll engage more. But the principle holds: engagement drives visibility faster than content creation.

And here's the beauty of this approach: it's sustainable.

Writing posts every day is exhausting. Finding something valuable to say five days a week is hard. But finding five great posts to comment on? That's easy. Those posts are already in your feed, written by people in your industry, sparking conversations you care about.

The 80/20 rule works because:

- Comments require less mental energy than posts

- You're leveraging other people's audiences instead of building your own from zero

- You're creating multiple touchpoints with the same effort it takes to write one post

- You're training the algorithm to show you more of the

content that matters

This is the shift that changes everything.
Stop thinking of LinkedIn as a publishing platform. Start thinking of it as a networking event.

At a networking event, you don't stand in the corner giving speeches. You join conversations. You add value to what other people are saying. You build relationships one interaction at a time. That's what strategic commenting is. And when you prioritize it over content creation, your visibility compounds faster than you'd think possible.

The Critical Distinction: Posts Build Authority, Comments Create Opportunity

If by now you are already seeing the value in commenting, you might be tempted to think that you should only comment and not create posts.

Let's be clear about something: You need both. Your posts and your comments serve different purposes. And if you only focus on one, you're leaving money on the table.

Your Posts = Authority Building

This is where you teach. Where you share frameworks, insights, and expertise. Where you establish yourself as the expert in your space.

Posts position you. They signal to the market what you know, what you believe, and what you stand for.

When someone clicks on your profile after seeing your comment, your posts are the proof. They back up the expertise you demonstrated in that comment.

Without posts, people see your comment and think, "Interesting take. But who is this person?" They click your profile and find... nothing. Or worse, a feed full of reposts and generic motivational quotes.

Content positions you as the expert. It's the long game.

Your Comments = Visibility & Door Opening

This is where you get seen. Where you start conversations. Where you turn strangers into connections and connections into clients.

Comments create opportunities. They get you in front of new audiences faster than any post ever will. They spark DMs, coffee chats, and client conversations.

When you comment strategically, you're not waiting for people to find you. You're showing up where they already are—engaged, interested, and reading.

Comments are the short game. The fast path to visibility.

Here's why you need both:

Content without engagement doesn't travel.

If you post great content but never engage, the algorithm won't prioritize your posts. LinkedIn rewards people who participate in conversations, not just those who start them.

Your posts will sit there, liked by the same 50 people who always like your stuff, never reaching new audiences.

Engagement without content leaves people wanting more.

If you comment brilliantly but have no posts on your profile, people will click through, see nothing, and move on.

You've demonstrated expertise in a comment, but there's no follow-through. No way for them to go deeper. No reason to connect or follow.

They'll think, "Smart comment," and forget about you five minutes later.

The strategy that works:

- Use comments to drive visibility and start conversations

- Use posts to establish authority and prove your expertise

Let them work together: comments bring people to your profile, posts convert them into followers or clients.

Think of it this way:
Comments are your handshake. They get you in the room.
Posts are your presentation. They prove you belong there.

You can't close a deal with just a handshake. But you'll never get the meeting without one.

The Takeaway

Before you type your next comment, ask yourself:
Am I doing this for visibility, credibility, or connection?

If the answer is "none of the above," don't waste your time. Strategic commenting isn't about being everywhere. It's about being in the right places with the right intention.

And when you get that right, everything else — the clients, the opportunities, the authority — follows.

Chapter Five

The Anatomy of an Expert Comment

Not all comments are created equal.

Some comments get you noticed. Some get you ignored. And some—the truly strategic ones—get you opportunities.

The difference isn't luck. It's structure.

An expert comment isn't just thoughtful—it's built to do something. It demonstrates expertise, adds value to the conversation, and positions you as someone worth paying attention to.

In this chapter, we're breaking down exactly what makes a comment work.

Write for the Poster, Position for the Feed

If you've ever hosted a hybrid event (some people in the room, some on Zoom) you know the challenge: you can't just talk to the people in front of you. You have to acknowledge both audiences, or one group feels ignored.

LinkedIn comments work the same way.
You're performing on two stages simultaneously:

Stage 1: The Original Poster

They're reading your comment directly. They need to feel seen, heard, valued. If you ignore them or just explain their own post back to them, you've lost the relationship. They won't respond, which means the algorithm won't amplify the conversation.

Stage 2: Everyone Scrolling Their Feed

Your comment shows up as standalone content in feeds. People who've never seen the original post will see YOUR comment. They're forming impressions about YOUR expertise. They might click through to YOUR profile without ever reading what you commented on.

Think of your comment as a mini-post, not a reaction.

Since comments now get their own reach and impressions count, substantial comments should be able to stand on their own and showcase your thinking. Here's what that means practically:

A good comment acknowledges the poster AND showcases your thinking for everyone else watching.

That's the foundation.
You're not just commenting but now you are creating content that happens to live in a comment section.

Now let's talk about how to craft a comment.

Over years of commenting, analyzing my own and watching thousands of others, I noticed a pattern. The comments that sparked real conversations, built real relationships, and led to actual opportunities weren't random. They weren't just thoughtful. They followed the same structure, every single time.

I built that structure into a framework.
I call The AICE ™ FRAMEWORK (pronounced "ACE And no, it has nothing to do with AI).

AICE stands for Attention, Insight, Credibility, and Engage. Master these four elements and you'll never leave a forgettable comment.

1. Attention

This is the opening line that makes people keep reading. This is your hook.

It could be:
1. A specific observation: "This happened to me last week."
2. A bold statement: "I'd actually push back on this."
3. A question: "Curious, have you seen this work in [specific scenario]?"
4. An agreement with nuance: "Yes, and I'd add one thing…"

This is where you capture attention. It signals that what comes next is worth reading.

The AICE™ Framework for Social Engagement

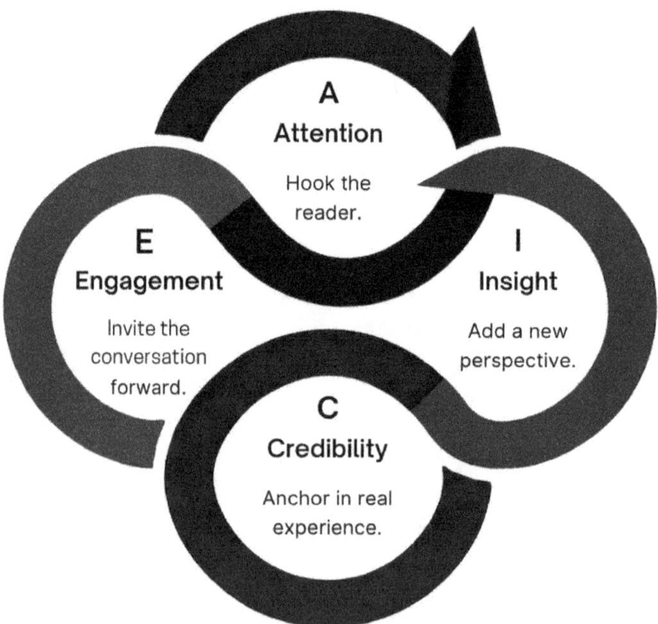

2. Insight

The fresh perspective. What you see that others missed. The nuance, connection, or angle that adds something new to the conversation.

This isn't just agreement or validation. It's your unique take—the pattern you've noticed, the connection you're making, the "yes, and..." that expands the original idea.

3. Credibility

This is where you prove you know what you're talking about.

Your credibility comes from your perspective, your experience, or your unique take on what the original poster said. It should be a substantive addition to the conversation.

Examples: - "In my experience, this works best when…" - "I've seen this fail when people skip the step of…" - "The nuance most people miss here is…"

This is what separates you from the "Great post!" crowd. It's proof you're actually thinking. You're sharing your lived experiences in real time.

4. Engagement

This is the value you add and how you keep the conversation going.

Engagement isn't just about dropping wisdom and walking away. It's about creating a reason for the conversation to continue. It's how you turn a single comment into a relationship.

This could be: - A question that invites their perspective - A specific example that adds depth to their point - A tactical next step that builds on what they shared - A genuine observation that opens dialogue - Continuing the conversation by engaging with other people's comments in the comment section

The engagement piece is what makes people remember you. It's what turns a comment into a connection, a connection into a conversation, and a conversation into a relationship.

Add, Don't Just Respond

When you see an educational post, add to it. Don't just respond to it.

There's a difference, and it matters more than most people realize.

Responding sounds like: "This is exactly what I needed to hear today."

Adding sounds like: "This is exactly what I needed to hear, and it reminded me of a pricing conversation I had with a client last week where we almost left $20K on the table because..."

See what happened there? The second one positions you as someone with experience. Someone who's lived it. The first positions you as an audience member. You're either in the room or you're watching from the seats. This one rule moves you to the front of the room.

Try to do this on at least 80–90% of your comments on educational content. Not every comment needs to be a masterclass. But most of them should add a layer, a perspective, a result, a "here's what I've seen," that makes the conversation richer because you showed up.

The Four Types of Strategic Comments

There are four comment structures that consistently work. Master these, and you'll never struggle with what to say.

Type 1: The "Add an Example" Comment

This comment takes the original post's idea and proves it with a real, specific example.

Original post: "Consistency beats perfection on LinkedIn."

Your comment:

"This hit home last week. I skipped posting because my idea wasn't polished enough. Then someone else shared the same thought and got 50+ comments. The lesson? Done beats perfect every time."

Why it works:

Personal, specific, and reinforces their point with real proof. You're not just agreeing—you're validating their idea with lived experience.

Type 2: The "Build On It" Comment

This comment takes the original idea deeper. You're not disagreeing, you're adding a layer of nuance or a tactical insight they didn't cover.

Original post: "Your offer needs to be clear."

Your comment:

"Here's the test: if you can't explain what you do in one sentence without buzzwords like 'holistic' or 'transformation,' it's not clear enough. I spent 6 months saying 'I help entrepreneurs grow' before realizing that means nothing."

Why it works:

Takes their idea deeper and adds tactical, actionable value. You're showing expertise by making their concept more useful.

Type 3: The "Respectful Counter-Perspective" Comment

This comment adds nuance by offering a different angle without being combative.

Original post: "Post daily to grow on LinkedIn."

Your comment:

"I'd add a caveat—daily posting works IF you have something valuable to say each day. I've seen people burn out posting just to hit a streak, and content quality tanks. Three strategic posts per week with real insights beats seven mediocre posts."

Why it works:

Shows independent thinking and adds nuance without being combative. You're not tearing them down—you're adding a necessary "but."

Type 4: The "Question That Advances Thinking" Comment

This comment asks a thoughtful question that invites deeper conversation—and shows you're thinking critically about the topic.

Original post: "Niching down is essential for business growth."

Your comment:

"Curious how you'd advise someone genuinely skilled in multiple areas? I see solopreneurs struggle with 'should I pick the thing I'm best at or the thing the market wants most?' What's been your experience?"

Why it works:

A thoughtful question invites deeper conversation and shows real engagement. You can invite conversations on the original post or on a comment.

The Strategic Use of Tags

Gyanda Sachdeva, LinkedIn's VP of Product Management, specifically mentioned tagging as a legitimate engagement tactic: "Adding meaningful perspectives, asking questions, or even tagging someone who might be able to add to the conversation is a great way to join the conversation."[1]

But here's the key phrase: someone who might be able to add to the conversation.

Tagging works when you're bringing relevant expertise or perspective into a discussion. It fails when you're using it as a distribution hack.

When to tag:

- You know someone with specific expertise on the topic being discussed
- You're giving credit to someone whose work you're referencing
- You're inviting someone whose perspective would genuinely enrich the conversation

When NOT to tag:

- Mass tagging multiple people to boost visibility
- Tagging your own clients or audience on someone else's post (that's hijacking)
- Tagging someone without a clear reason why they'd benefit from seeing it

The test: Would the person you're tagging genuinely benefit from seeing this post and joining this conversation, or would they think "Why did I get dragged into this?"

If it's the latter, don't tag.

The Comment Hierarchy: Supportive → Insightful → Authoritative

Not every comment needs to be a masterpiece. Some comments are just about showing up and being supportive.

But if you want to build authority, you need to understand the hierarchy.

Level 1: Supportive Comments

These are the "Great post!" and "Thanks for sharing!" comments.

They're not strategic. They're not memorable. But they're not always wrong.

When supportive comments work: - When you're engaging with a 1st-degree connection and you just want to show up - When the post is a personal win or celebration and a thoughtful comment would feel performative - When you genuinely don't have anything substantive to add but want to signal support

Supportive comments are fine in moderation. But they don't build credibility. They're the LinkedIn equivalent of a polite nod.

Level 2: Insightful Comments

These are the comments that add something—an example, a perspective, a question.

They show you're paying attention. They demonstrate that you understand the topic. They make people think, "This person gets it."

Insightful comments build visibility and credibility simultaneously.

When to use insightful comments: - When commenting on 2nd-degree connections or industry influencers - When the post is about a topic you have experience with - When you want to get noticed by the original poster or their audience

This is your bread and butter. Most of your strategic comments should fall into this category.

Level 3: Authoritative Comments

These are the comments that make people stop, screenshot, and send to their colleagues.

They're not just insightful—they're definitive. They demonstrate mastery. They position you as someone who doesn't just understand the topic—they've lived it, taught it, and have strong opinions about it.

When to use authoritative comments: - When the post is directly in your lane of expertise - When you're commenting on a high-visibility post and want to stand out - When you're building a case for why someone should hire you

Authoritative comments are powerful. But use them sparingly. If every comment you write is a dissertation, you'll come across as trying too hard.

The goal is to move up the hierarchy strategically—not to stay stuck at "Great post!" forever.

What Makes a Comment Forgettable

Before we talk about what to do, let's be clear about what NOT to do.

These comments waste your time and some can damage your credibility:

1. "This is so important!"

You repeat what they said without adding anything new to the conversation.

2. "I help businesses with this. DM me!"

Gross self-promotion disguised as engagement. Nobody wants this on their post.

3. The "Agree and Disappear" Trap

This is when you say "I agree" and... nothing else.

If all you're doing is agreeing, you're not adding value. You're just taking up space in the comment section. Your comment effectively blends into the background and disappears.

Why LinkedIn Stopped Rewarding Generic Comments

For years, LinkedIn's algorithm was simple: more comments = more reach.

People figured this out quickly. Engagement pods formed; groups of users agreeing to like and comment on each other's posts regardless of relevance. The result? Comment sections filled with "Great post!" and empty praise designed to game the system, not to add value.

LinkedIn's Editor in Chief, Dan Roth, explained the shift in a 2024 interview with Entrepreneur magazine's Jason Feifer:

"In the past, LinkedIn would amplify posts that got a lot of comments. As a result, some users banded together into 'engagement groups'—essentially agreeing to quickly like and comment on each other's posts, as a way of boosting them. LinkedIn wanted to stop that. Now it rewards posts that get what Roth calls 'meaningful comments.' This means that people aren't just dashing off empty comments—stuff like 'great!' or 'so true!'—but are instead actually responding to the content of the post."

Here's what changed:

LinkedIn no longer cares about comment volume. They care about comment quality.

Roth clarified:

"There is advice from LinkedIn gurus telling people they need a lot of comments and that's not true. You don't need a lot of comments, you need relevant ones that result in a dialogue."

And here's the critical piece most people miss:

It's not enough to leave a thoughtful comment. Roth emphasized that post authors need to engage back:

"You also need to reply to the comments, so that you don't just broadcast your content, but actually have meaningful conversations with your audience."[2]

This is why the Comment Currency framework works:

It's built around meaningful engagement, not volume

Every comment adds insight, not just agreement

We prioritize dialogue both in comments we leave AND comments we respond to

No automation, no gaming the system, no engagement pods

LinkedIn's algorithm evolved to reward exactly what we're teaching: strategic, authentic, value-driven commenting that sparks real conversation.

Never Hijack Someone's Post

Here's a hard rule: Don't make someone else's post about you.

This is the fastest way to burn a bridge and kill your credibility.

Let's break down the most common ways people hijack posts and how to avoid them.

Hijack #1: The "Let Me Tell MY Story" Comment

Original post: "Just landed my first $10K client! Here's what worked…"

Bad comment:

"Congrats! I remember when I landed my first big client back in 2019. I was working with this tech startup and here's what I did…" [proceeds to write 300 words about themselves]

Why it's hijacking:

You just made their win about you. Nobody cares about your story in THEIR moment.

Good comment instead:

"This is huge—congrats! That first $10K client is a game-changer because it proves your value at that level. What surprised you most about the sales conversation compared to smaller deals?"

Why it works:

Celebrates them, keeps the spotlight where it belongs, and asks a thoughtful question that lets them share more.

Hijack #2: The "Actually, Here's the REAL Answer" Comment

Original post: "Here are 3 ways to improve your LinkedIn headline."

Bad comment:

"I'd actually add that the MOST important thing is..." [lists 5 completely different strategies and rewrites their entire post]

Why it's hijacking:

You're positioning yourself as the expert (good) and undermining their authority on their own post (bad).

Good comment instead:

"Love these. I'd add one more layer-tying your headline directly to the pain point your ideal client is searching for. Makes it easier for the right people to find you."

Why it works:

You're adding to what they said, not replacing it.

Hijack #3: The "I Do This Too! Here's My Approach" Comment

Original post: "My framework for client onboarding."

Bad comment:

"Great minds! I do something similar but I also include…" [writes their entire different framework]

Why it's hijacking:

You're competing with them on their own post instead of supporting their message.

Good comment instead:

"The step you outlined about setting expectations upfront is critical. I've seen so many client relationships go sideways because that piece was skipped."

Why it works:

You're reinforcing their framework, not pitching your own.

Hijack #4: The "Let Me Correct You" Comment

Example: Someone posts "You need to switch from an LLC to an S Corporation for tax benefits!"

Don't comment:

"Actually, this is incorrect. An S Corp is just a tax election, not a business structure…"

Your only options:
1. DM them privately with the correction
2. Say nothing publicly

Why?

If it's important enough to correct, it deserves a private message. If not, it's definitely not worth a public comment.

Public corrections make you look like you're trying to one-up them. Private corrections make you look like someone who cares about helping.

Hijack #5: The "Check Out My Link" Comment

Original post: Any post from someone else

Bad comment:

"Great point! I wrote about this too: [link to your article/post/website]"

Why it's hijacking:

You're redirecting their audience to YOUR content. It's self-serving and looks desperate.

Your only options: 1. Comment without the link and add value on their post 2. If your content genuinely helps, DM them privately with the link

Why?

Links in comments on someone else's post are a hard no. It signals you're using their post as free advertising. Even if your content is relevant, it comes across as self-promotional.

If your insight is valuable, share it directly in the comment. The value speaks for itself—no link needed.

Good Comments Are Specific, Add Value, and Prove You're Thinking

Let's talk about what all the good examples have in common:

They're specific.

Not "Great post!" but "This specific part resonated because…"

They add genuine value.

They give an example, build on the idea, or ask a thoughtful question.

They prove you're actually thinking.

You're engaging with the content at a deeper level.

When you comment strategically, you're not trying to be everywhere. You're trying to be memorable.

And memorable comes from being specific, valuable, and thoughtful.

The Takeaway

Before you type your next comment, ask yourself:

Does this comment do one of these four things?
1. Add an example

2. Build on the idea
3. Offer a respectful counter-perspective
4. Ask a question that advances thinking

If the answer is no, don't post it.

Your comments are your calling card. They're how people decide whether you're worth paying attention to.

Make them count.

---

1. [1] Gyanda Sachdeva, VP of Product Management at LinkedIn, has stated publicly that adding meaningful perspectives, asking questions, and tagging relevant voices are among the best ways to engage on the platform.

2. Dan Roth, Editor in Chief at LinkedIn, interviewed by Jason Feifer. "With This LinkedIn Algorithm Change, Your Best Posts Could Reach New Readers for Months."
Entrepreneur, February 2024.
https://www.entrepreneur.com/science-technology/with-this-linkedin-algorithm-change-your-best-posts-could/470219

PART III

BUILDING YOUR VISIBILITY SYSTEM

Chapter Six

The Daily Commenting Routine

Your 15 Minutes That Change Everything

You know LinkedIn works for business growth. You know it can be a gold mine.

But if you are like most people, you don't have hours to spend on LinkedIn. You have a business to run, clients to serve, revenue to generate.

The good news? You don't need hours. You need 15 minutes.

Not 15 minutes of scrolling. Not 15 minutes of passive liking. 15 minutes of strategic, focused engagement that builds relationships, demonstrates expertise, and creates visibility. The reason 15 minutes is enough? You're not guessing what to say, you have the AICE framework.

Here's what that looks like in practice:

The Minimum Viable Routine (10 minutes when you're slammed):

- 3-4 strategic comments using the AICE framework
- Quick check-back later for any replies
- Done

The Standard Routine (15 minutes, most days):
- 5-6 strategic comments using the AICE framework
- 5 minutes responding to replies on your own comments
- Done

The Expanded Routine (30 minutes when you have bandwidth or a non-negotiable as you grow):
- 8-10 strategic comments using the AICE framework
- 10 minutes responding to replies and starting conversations
- 5 minutes mining comment sections for new people to add to your list
- Done

Why consistency beats volume:

You could comment on 50 posts today and then disappear for two weeks. The algorithm won't reward that. Your network won't remember you. And you'll burn out.

Or you could comment on 5 posts today, 5 tomorrow, 5 the next day. The algorithm will notice. Your network will recognize your name. And you'll build a sustainable habit that actually works.

Consistency isn't sexy. But it compounds.
Five AICE comments a day beats fifty throwaway comments every time

Pick Your Time (And Stick to It)

Here's what most people get wrong: they think commenting only works if you do it during "peak hours" or first thing in the morning when posts are fresh.

Not true.

The algorithm doesn't care WHEN you engage. It cares THAT you engage consistently.

Not a morning person? Good. This system works anytime.

The key isn't finding the perfect time—it's picking YOUR time and showing up at that time most days. The consistency is what trains both the algorithm and your brain.

Pick your window: - Morning coffee ritual (before the workday chaos starts) - Lunch break (when you need a mental reset) - Evening wind-down (after you've closed your laptop for client work) - Whenever works for your schedule and energy

Why the same time matters:

When you comment at roughly the same time each day, it becomes automatic. You don't have to decide, "Should I engage today?" or "When should I do this?" Your brain knows: 8am with coffee = LinkedIn commenting. Done.

Random engagement doesn't build momentum. You'll forget. You'll skip days. You'll talk yourself out of it when you're busy.

The rule: Pick a time that's realistic for your life. If mornings are chaos with kids and client calls, don't force morning engagement. If evenings are when you finally have brain space, that's your window.

Consistency beats optimization every single time.

On Days When You're Posting

If it's a day you're publishing your own content, your routine shifts slightly.**Step 1: Warm up the algorithm**

Start with 2-3 strategic comments on other people's posts. This signals to LinkedIn that you're active and engaging, which helps your post get better initial distribution.

Step 2: Publish your post

Step 3: Go back to commenting

Don't post and ghost. Continue with your remaining 3 – 4 comments on other people's content.

Step 4: Respond to comments on your own post

Make sure you respond to every comment on your own post. This is non-negotiable.

Step 5: Circle back and check your post

Set a reminder to check your notifications or revisit your post later in the day.This ensures you're not just posting and disappearing. LinkedIn rewards creators who participate in conversations, not only those who publish content.

CALLOUT:Pro tip: LinkedIn defaults to showing comments sorted by "Most relevant." This means you might miss new comments. Change the sort to "Most recent" and you'll see who has recently commented, so you can respond promptly.

Responding quickly shows you're present, keeps the conversation going, and signals to the algorithm that your post is generating real engagement.

Even LinkedIn Thinks Commenting Is Important

LinkedIn now shows you stats on your individual comments—impressions, likes, and replies. Think about that: LinkedIn built infrastructure to track and display metrics for comments, not just posts. They're telling you what matters. If commenting wasn't valuable, they wouldn't be measuring it. Pay attention to which comments get traction. That's data showing you what resonates with your audience.

Organize Your List First

Before you start your daily routine, you need to solve one critical problem: How do you actually find the posts from your 15 people without scrolling through your entire feed?

LinkedIn's algorithm shows you what IT thinks you want to see—not necessarily what you NEED to see. You could spend 10 minutes just looking for posts from the people you actually want to engage with.

That's where these two systems come in. Pick the one that works for your brain, or use both.

The Bookmark Hack #1 (Kevin D. Turner System)

I first learned this from Kevin. It is a great way to see posts from people you want to see posts from.

Here's how it works:

Step 1: Go to the LinkedIn search bar and click "Posts" (first dropdown option)

Step 2: Click "Sort by: Latest" so you see the most recent content first

Step 3: Choose your time frame - "Past 24 hours" or "Past week" depending on how often you engage

Step 4: Click "Posted by member" and start typing the names of people you've identified for your list. Add them one by one to the search.

Step 5: Click "Show results"

Now you're looking at a custom feed showing ONLY posts from those specific people. No algorithm. No random content. Just the people you chose.

Step 6: Bookmark this page in your browser.

That's the hack. LinkedIn won't save this search for you, but your browser will.

Every time you click that bookmark, it loads the exact same custom feed—posts from your curated list of people, sorted by latest, ready for you to engage.

Here's where it gets powerful:

You can create multiple bookmarks for different lists:

Bookmark 1: "Ideal Clients" - 10-15 potential clients you want to build relationships with

Bookmark 2: "Industry Influencers" - 5-10 people with large, relevant audiences

Bookmark 3: "Referral Partners" - 10-15 people who serve your same audience with complementary services

Each bookmark is a different custom feed. Each one opens in seconds.

Optional: Organize these bookmarks into a browser bookmark folder (Chrome, Safari, Firefox all have this) labeled "LinkedIn Engagement" so they're all in one place.

Why this changes everything:

When you sit down for your 15-minute daily commenting session, you don't scroll aimlessly hoping to find the right posts. You open your bookmark, and BAM, there's a feed full of exactly the people you want to engage with.

No distractions. No algorithm guessing. Just strategic, intentional engagement.

The Bookmark Hack #2 (Tab System)

I'm one of those people who have 12 windows open and each one of those windows has 92 tabs (almost not exaggerating). I feel that if I close the tab I'm going to lose information or forget to circle back to it. But most browsers have "groups." This has been instrumental to keeping my obsession with so many tabs open manageable.

Think of tab groups like a notebook with sections. The sections are a little tab that tells you what the section is about. When you open the tab group, all the windows or tabs within it open at once. So you can choose the section or profile that you want to comment on.

You would create a tab group for:

ICA (Ideal Client Avatar) - The people you want as clients

Peers & Potential Collaborators - Strategic relationships, referral partners, people you'd work with

People You Champion - People you genuinely want to support (no agenda)

Influencers - People in your field or who share your ICA that you want to learn from and engage with

How to set this up:

Open LinkedIn profiles for each person in a category, then use your browser's tab grouping feature (Chrome, Safari, Edge all have this) to save them as a group. Name the groups accordingly.

A Word About That Fourth Group (Influencers)

If you're not first to comment, your comments can get buried. That being said, I have successfully left comments that have started conversations even when I was comment number 597. Remember too, LinkedIn now shows you impressions on your comments, but expect more engagement when you comment first and your comment gets that boost of initial engagement.

The beauty of this system: You never scroll aimlessly. You open a tab group, engage with intention, close it. Done.

This allows you to be very specific about people. If you want to be very specific and not scroll through to see their posts, it's more efficient when you have less time and you're like, "OK, I want to hit boom boom boom—this person, this person, this person." Done.

Now, you still need to spend time finding others. You don't want it to get stale. You need to keep expanding your circle. But on days when time is limited? Boom. Done.

Pick the method that works for your brain. Or use both; for example you can bookmark searches for broad categories and then tab groups for your core 15 people you engage with every single day.

Your Daily Workflow

Now that you've picked your time and organized your list, here's what you actually do during your commenting session.

On Days You DON'T Post

Step 1: Open your system (30 seconds)

Open your bookmarks or tab groups. You're starting with a curated feed of exactly the people you want to engage with—no scrolling, no distractions.

Step 2: Scan for posts (2 minutes)

Quickly scan through the posts from your list. You're looking for posts where you have something substantive to add.

Step 3: Choose your 5-6 posts (1 minute)

Pick the posts you'll comment on.

What to prioritize: - Posts from your ICA group (these are the people you want as clients) - Posts with fewer than 10 comments (you won't get buried) - Posts from peers where your ICA is already engaging - You can engage with the post or engage with the comments already on the post (or both, depending)

Step 4: Write your comments (10 minutes)

For each comment, try to use the AICE framework from chapter 5:
- Attention: Your opening that makes people want to read further
- Insight: The fresh perspective or new angle you bring
- Credibility: Your lived experience or perspective that backs it up
- Engagement: The invitation to continue the conversation

Step 5: Post your comments

Hit "Comment" on each one. The algorithm sees the engagement and realizes this is a post worth sharing.

Step 6: Set a reminder to check back (later that day)

Set a reminder for 3-4 hours later to check notifications for replies on your comments. You don't need to live on

LinkedIn, but you do need to respond when people engage with you. That's how comments become conversations.

On Days You DO Post

Step 1: Warm up the algorithm (5 minutes)

Step 2: Publish your post

Step 3: Go back to commenting (5 minutes)

Step 4: Respond to comments on your own post (5 minutes)

Respond to every comment on your own post. The algorithm sees this engagement and realizes this is a post worth sharing.

The Pinned Comment Strategy

Your own comment section is real estate. Right after you publish, post a pinned comment. It sits at the top so it's the first thing people see when they engage. It's a second swing at the conversation, a chance to go deeper, add context, or direct people somewhere useful.

And here's what the data shows: pinned comments increase dwell time. When people stick around to read the comments, and especially when they engage there too, LinkedIn reads that as a signal that your content is worth spreading. More dwell time, more distribution.

So what do you pin? Here are the ones I use most: - Bonus points — something useful that didn't fit in the main post - Fun facts or stats — a screenshot, a data point, something visual - A question — open it up, invite a response, run a quick AMA - Behind the scenes — what happened before or after the post's topic - Announcements or offers — the comment section is a much better place for links than the post itself - A repost call-to-action — if the content deserves a wider audience, ask for it

You put the work into the post. Don't abandon it the second you hit publish. Show up in your own comment section like you would in anyone else's, with intention.

Step 5: Circle back and check your post

Set a reminder to check your notifications or revisit your post later in the day.

Start Small, Build Up

If 15 minutes feels overwhelming, start with 10. If 5-6 comments feels like too much, start with 3. Like anything else, it gets easier as you do it more. The system becomes second nature. Your comments get faster to write. You'll know what resonates. Give yourself permission to ease into this.

That's it. 15 minutes. Done.

You've just: - Demonstrated your expertise to exactly the right people - Built relationships in real time - Created visibility without posting a single thing

Tomorrow, you'll do it again. And the day after that. This is how consistency compounds.

Chapter Seven

Building Conversations

The Follow-Up

You've left your 5-6 comments. You've moved on with your day. Now what?

This is where most people drop the ball. They comment, they leave, and they never come back. The conversation dies. The opportunity dies with it.

The 3-4 hour check-in:

Set a reminder (phone, calendar, whatever works) to check your LinkedIn notifications 3-4 hours after your commenting session.

You're looking for:
- Replies to your comments
- Likes on your comments (these matter—someone noticed)
- The original poster responding to you - Other commenters engaging with what you said

What to do when someone replies:

Respond. Even if it's simple.

If they ask a question, answer it. If they add to your point, acknowledge it. If they disagree respectfully, engage with their perspective. If they leave an emoji you can like it or leave one back. This doesn't have to be another full AICE comment. A genuine 1-2 sentence reply keeps the conversation alive.

Example:

Their reply: "This is such a good point. I hadn't thought about it that way."

Your response can end the conversation chain: "Glad it resonated!"

Or keep it going: "Glad it resonated! What's been your experience with this?" Keeps the conversation going (that's if they respond).

Why this matters:

When you reply to someone's comment on YOUR comment, LinkedIn sees ongoing engagement. The algorithm rewards conversations, not one-sided monologues. Plus, this is how you turn a comment thread into a DM, a DM into a coffee chat, a coffee chat into a client.

The reality check:

You won't always get replies. Some comments just sit there. Sometimes people don't check their notifications and don't realize that somebody else has responded to their comment.

That's fine. The visibility happened. The demonstration of expertise happened. Not every comment turns into a conversation, and that's okay.

But when someone DOES reply? Show up. That's when the real relationship building begins.

End-of-day sweep (optional):

Before you close your laptop for the day, do one final check. Reply to any stragglers. Check your own posts if you published that day.

This takes 5 minutes. Maybe less. But it closes the loop and ensures you're not leaving people hanging.

The 1+3 Strategy

I learned this one from Jasmin Alić. This strategy quietly builds relationships, and has created incredible business opportunities for me on LinkedIn.

The strategy is simple:

1 strong comment + 3 thoughtful replies.

Here's how it works.

You find a post worth engaging with and leave a strong comment — something that actually adds to the conversation, often using the AICE framework.

But you don't stop there.

Refresh the post. Scroll through the other comments. Look for people who match your ICP (your ideal clients), as well as collaborators and peers, the people you want in your world.

Then reply to **three of their comments**.

Not a generic "great point!" reply, but an intentional one that continues the thread, adds perspective, or opens the door to a real conversation.

That's the 1+**3**.

1 strong comment that creates visibility + 3 strategic replies that build relationships

Here's why it works: the original post has already pulled your people in. They're right there — commenting, engaged, and participating in a conversation you're now part of.

Replying to their comments isn't cold outreach. It's a warm, natural extension of a conversation that's already happening. Do this consistently and watch how quickly names become familiar — and how often those familiar names end up in your DMs.

From Comment to Client

Most opportunities follow a simple path:

Comment → Micro-conversation in the thread → DM →
Call → Offer.

Once a comment has turned into a real exchange —
you've gone back and forth at least once or twice, or
the other person has clearly signaled interest — you can
gently bridge the conversation.

For example:

- "This is exactly the kind of thing I help clients with.
  If you'd like, I'm happy to take a quick look at your
  situation and share a few ideas — no pressure."

- "I have a simple framework for this that might save
  you some trial and error. Want me to send you a
  short video or walk you through it on a quick call?"

- "If you're exploring this seriously, I offer a focused
  session where we map out your LinkedIn visibility
  plan in 60 minutes. If that would be helpful, I can
  send you the details."

**The goal is not to sell in the comments. The goal is
to earn enough trust in public that an invitation to
continue the conversation in private feels natural... not
pushy.**

***When you've shown up consistently with value, that
invitation is often exactly what people are hoping you'll
offer.***

Chapter Eight

What To Do When Life Gets Busy

The Best Laid Plans...

Life doesn't care about your LinkedIn commenting routine.

You'll get slammed with client work. You'll have family emergencies. You'll travel. You'll get sick. You'll have weeks where you're barely keeping your head above water, let alone thinking about strategic engagement.

This is normal. This is reality.

The people who succeed with Comment Currency aren't the ones who never miss a day. They're the ones who adjust when life gets messy and get back on track when things settle down.

Here's how to make this sustainable.

The 3-Tier System

You don't need to be at 100% all the time. You need three modes you can shift between based on what's happening in your life.

Full Engagement Mode (30 minutes/day)

- 8-10 strategic comments

- 10 minutes responding to replies and starting conversations

- 5 minutes mining comment sections for new people

- This is when you have bandwidth and you're building momentum

Maintenance Mode (15 minutes/day)

- 5-6 strategic comments

- 5 minutes responding to replies

- This is your standard routine—the one you can sustain most days

Survival Mode (10 minutes/day)

- 3-4 strategic comments on your ICA tab only

- Quick check for replies, respond if urgent - This is when life is chaos and you're doing the absolute minimum to stay visible

A note on quick comments: If you don't have time to do the full AICE comment, at least make sure you're leaving valuable quick comments. And by valuable, I don't mean "Hey, great post!" I mean something with a little thought behind it. Perhaps not as strategic as AICE, but still substantive. "This happened to me last week" or "The nuance I'd add here..." - something that shows you're actually thinking.

The key: Communicate with yourself about which mode you're in. Don't beat yourself up for being in Survival Mode. Don't try to operate in Full Engagement when you're drowning.

Pick the mode that matches your reality, and execute it. That's better than burning out or disappearing entirely.

When It's Important Enough, You Make the Time

On the other end of the spectrum are the people who treat engagement as non-negotiable.

I've watched people travel internationally and still get up early so they could post at the same time they always post and respond to comments before their day began.

I've seen them check back throughout the day, continuing the conversation even while traveling.

For them, engagement isn't something they do when they have time.It's something they protect time for.

You don't need to go to that extreme. But you do need to decide:

Is this important enough to protect?

If the answer is yes, find 10 minutes. Even on the hard days.

My Reality

My business goes in cycles. Sometimes I'm really busy and sometimes I'm not. But every day I will get on LinkedIn and leave at least 5 quick comments. They don't always follow the AICE framework, but I'm showing up in the spaces that matter to me.

That's the real secret: show up. Even when it's messy. Even when it's not perfect.

The algorithm rewards consistency. Your network rewards presence. And your business rewards visibility.

Do what you can with what you have. That's enough.

If you follow this system (bookmarking strategic people, focusing on 15 at a time, and engaging with intention) you won't waste time, energy, or effort engaging with the wrong posts. You'll naturally avoid engagement bait, overcrowded threads, and random viral content. You're not scrolling. You're not reacting. You're being strategic.

Chapter Nine

Finding the Right People

Mining Comment Sections for New People

Here's the truth: your ideal clients aren't just scrolling their feed waiting for you to show up. They're already engaging somewhere. They're commenting on posts. They're having conversations. They're showing up in places you might not be looking.

Your people are already gathering somewhere.

And it's usually not in your inbox. It's not in your DMs. It's in the comment sections of:

People talking about what you talk about - Industry peers, thought leaders, educators in your space

People serving the same audience you serve - Adjacent service providers, complementary businesses

People doing adjacent work in your space - Not direct competitors, but people working with the same problems from a different angle

How to mine comment sections:

When you're engaging on a post from someone in your field or someone who serves your ICA, don't just comment and leave. Scroll through the other comments.

Look for people who are: - Asking smart questions - Adding thoughtful perspectives - Demonstrating they understand the problem you solve - Engaging respectfully and substantively (not just "Great post! ")

These are your people.

What to do when you find them:

Click their profile. Check if they match your ICA or could be a strategic peer/collaborator. If yes, add them to your rotation list.

You can engage with their comment right there in the thread (this introduces you to them AND the original poster), and/or you can connect with them and start engaging with their content directly.

The key principle: Don't hijack, but support.

You're not there to steal attention from the original poster. You're there to support peers in your industry AND find the people who are already engaged in the conversations that matter to your business.

Look through their comments. Find your people there.

Supporting New Voices

You're not just looking for the biggest names or the most established creators. Some of the best engagement comes from supporting newer creators who are posting quality content but don't have traction yet.

Creating content is hard. Being early to someone's work matters. And it's really easy to support somebody and cheer them on by engaging with them.

Plus, they remember who showed up when they had 47 followers and no comments. Today's new creator is tomorrow's superstar, maybe simply because you supported them.

Section 7: When to Expand Your List

Your 15-person list isn't permanent. It's a living system that evolves with your business and your network.

Signs it's time to rotate:

You're getting stale. The same people, the same topics, the same conversations. You're not learning anything new, and you're not reaching new audiences.

Engagement is dropping. Your comments used to spark conversations. Now they're getting polite likes but no real interaction.

Your business has shifted. You're targeting a different ICA, selling a different offer, or positioning yourself differently. Your list should reflect that.

You've maxed out the relationship. You've been engaging consistently with someone for months. They know you exist. They respond when you comment. They never comment on yours (so there is no reciprocal). The visibility work is done. Time to make room for new connections.

When to add people:

You found them in comment sections and they're consistently showing up with smart perspectives

They're posting content that resonates with your ICA

They're in your field or serve your audience and you want to build a relationship

They're newer creators posting quality content who could use the support

As you rotate out people, you may want to keep them on an occasional engagement list. You can now even create another bookmark for your occasional engagement list. Replace "stale" profiles with new people you've found and move those you're rotating out onto your occasional engagement list.

The cadence:

Review your list every 4-6 weeks. Ask yourself: - Are these still the right 15 people? - Who's missing? - Who should I phase out? - Who should I add?

Your goal isn't to churn through people. It's to keep your network growing while maintaining strategic focus.

Comments to Conversations: The DM Bridge

Not every comment needs to become a DM. In fact, most shouldn't.

But when a conversation in the comments is genuinely building momentum, there's a natural moment to take it private. Here's how to know when.

The Traffic Light System

Green Light = clear buying signal or explicit invitation to continue the conversation

- They've replied to your comment 2+ times with substantive responses

- They've asked YOU a question

- They've said something like "I'd love to hear more about this" or "We should continue this conversation"

Go Ahead and DM

Yellow Light = maybe DM if you have a clear, specific reason that serves them.

- One thoughtful reply, but no clear invitation to continue

- They engaged, but it feels complete

Proceed with Caution

Red Light = do not DM (purely transactional, no rapport)

- No reply at all

- Generic "Thanks!" or "Appreciate this"

They're being polite, not interested

When you do DM:

- Don't pitch immediately. Reference the conversation, don't pivot to your offer.

- Don't ask to "pick their brain." It signals you want to extract value without giving any.

- Don't make it about YOU getting something. Continue the conversation, don't hijack it for your agenda.

- The best DMs feel like a natural continuation of what you were already discussing. If it feels forced, it probably is.

PART IV
360BREW AND WHY IT MATTERS

Chapter Ten

The Algorithm Just Got Smarter

I n January 2025, LinkedIn launched 360Brew, a unified AI foundation model that fundamentally changed how content gets distributed on the platform.

This isn't just an algorithm update. This is LinkedIn replacing its entire patchwork of older, simpler algorithms with one large-scale AI model that can actually read and understand what you're saying.

What Changed

Old LinkedIn (pre-360Brew): - Multiple separate algorithms: one for feed, one for jobs, one for "People You May Know" - Heavy reliance on keywords, hashtags, recency, and quick engagement spikes - Surface-level signals: did this post get likes fast? Did it use the right keywords?

New LinkedIn (with 360Brew): - One unified model (tens of billions of parameters) powering everything - Reads semantic meaning: what you're actually saying, not just keywords - Evaluates your long-term expertise patterns, not just individual posts - Scores how clearly you express ideas and how well topics fit your established authority

Here's the shift that matters most:

360Brew doesn't just look at what you post today. It looks at your entire pattern: your profile positioning, your posting history, your interactions, your consistency over time.

It's training itself to recognize you as a credible specialist in specific topics. Not as a general influencer. As an expert in 2-3 clear areas.

What 360Brew Rewards

What matters MORE now:

Clear professional positioning (headline, About section, consistent themes)
2-3 main topics you talk about consistently over time
Quality writing with depth and structure that keeps people reading
Thoughtful comments that add real insight
Meaningful engagement (dwell time, substantive replies, saves, shares)

What matters LESS now:

Posting every day just to stay active
Hashtags and keyword stuffing
Vanity engagement tactics (pods, shallow reactions)
Viral spikes without topical relevance

The Research Backs It Up

This isn't just a strategy. It's a documented shift.

Richard van der Blom, LinkedIn strategist and algorithm expert, has tracked this evolution extensively through his annual Algorithm Insights Report / Content & Algorithm Playbook, one of the most cited research resources in the LinkedIn community.

His findings are direct: comments of 15 or more words significantly boost reach. Insight-driven comment threads get resurfaced for weeks. And while posting once a day shows you once to your existing network, leaving 10 to 15 strategic comments shows you 10 to 15 times across entirely different networks, multiplying your profile views, follower growth, and inbound opportunities.

He put it simply:

"Commenting is the new posting." [1]

That's a data-backed conclusion from someone who has spent years measuring exactly how LinkedIn distributes content and rewards engagement.

Dan Roth, Editor in Chief of LinkedIn, often talks about the power of commenting:

"Commenting is like giving back. When you post, sometimes you're like, 'Is this resonating with anyone?' And the comment is someone raising their hand. The comment is someone saying, 'I loved what you said' or 'Made me think about this or that.' If you think about commenting as a way of helping the original poster feel better about what they're saying, that makes it a lot easier."[2]

Why Comment Currency Works WITH 360Brew

Here's the beautiful thing: everything you've learned in this book is exactly what 360Brew rewards.

Your daily routine:

- Consistent engagement in your niche (builds your expertise pattern)

- Strategic focus on 15 people (depth over breadth)

- Thoughtful comments over volume (quality signals)

Your positioning:

- Clear about who you serve and what you know

- Consistent themes in your engagement

- Building authority in specific areas, not trying to be everything to everyone

Why AICE Is Built for 360Brew

AICE wasn't designed around LinkedIn's algorithm. But when 360Brew launched, something became clear — every element of the framework maps directly to what the algorithm is now designed to reward.

This isn't a coincidence. It's proof that strategic commenting, done right, has always been aligned with what LinkedIn actually wants from its platform.

Here's how it connects:

Attention — 360Brew measures dwell time. How long someone stops on a piece of content before scrolling past. A strong opening line earns that pause. A weak one gets skipped. Every time you write an opening that makes someone stop, you're sending exactly the signal 360Brew is listening for.

Insight — The algorithm evaluates depth and context, not just keywords. Generic takes get deprioritized. Fresh perspective, nuance, and original thinking get amplified. When you add something new to a conversation instead of just validating what's already there, 360Brew notices.

Credibility — This is where it gets powerful. 360Brew doesn't just look at individual comments or posts. It builds a picture of you over time — your topics, your consistency, your expertise patterns across all your activity. Every credibility signal you leave in a comment trains the algorithm to recognize your authority.

Engagement — Meaningful replies, saves, and continued conversation are the signals 360Brew weighs most heavily. Not reactions. Not empty likes. Real back-and-forth. The engagement element of AICE isn't just relationship-building — it's the exact behavior the algorithm is designed to amplify.

You're not gaming the system. You're giving 360Brew exactly what it's designed to amplify: genuine expertise, consistent value, real relationships.

The Playing Field Just Got More Level

People who've been gaming LinkedIn with engagement pods, keyword stuffing, and manufactured visibility? Their reach is dropping. For now
People who show up with real expertise and genuine engagement? Their visibility is increasing. not necessarily in volume, but in front of the people who actually matter: potential clients, referral partners, and peers who recognize real expertise when they see it.

360Brew can tell the difference between:

- A thoughtful comment that adds perspective vs. "Great post!"
- Genuine conversation vs. coordinated pod engagement
- Real expertise vs. generic advice
- Consistent authority in a niche vs. scattered random content

This is why strategic commenting works even better now than before.

The Human Advantage

AI can generate content. It can write posts, create graphics, even draft comments.

But AI can't replicate your lived experience. It can't share the specific lesson you learned from that client project that went sideways. It can't tell the story of the strategy that failed three times before it finally worked.

Your real perspective (your actual expertise, your genuine insights, your specific examples) is your competitive advantage.

And 360Brew knows the difference.

When you comment with real experience, the algorithm recognizes it. When you add genuine value to a conversation, the algorithm amplifies it. When you build consistent patterns of expertise through your engagement, the algorithm rewards it.

Future-Proofing Your Strategy

LinkedIn's algorithm will keep evolving. 360Brew will get smarter at reading context, detecting fake engagement, and surfacing quality.

But here's what won't change: LinkedIn wants real professionals having real conversations in their areas of expertise.
That's what ***Comment Currency*** is built on.

You're not chasing algorithmic hacks. You're not exploiting loopholes. You're showing up consistently, sharing genuine expertise, building real relationships in your niche. The algorithm rewarded that before 360Brew. It rewards it even more now. And it will reward it five years from now.

What This Means for You

If you follow the ***Comment Currency*** system:
- Your consistent engagement trains 360Brew to recognize your expertise
- Your thoughtful comments signal quality over vanity metrics
- Your strategic focus on specific people and topics builds your authority pattern
- Your genuine relationships create the meaningful engagement signals that matter

You're not fighting the algorithm. You're working with it.

The Bottom Line

360Brew doesn't change the Comment Currency strategy.

It validates it.

Everything in this book (the AICE framework, the daily routine, the focus on quality over quantity, the emphasis on genuine relationships, the consistency over perfection) is exactly what LinkedIn's algorithm is designed to amplify.

Keep showing up. Keep adding value. Keep building real relationships in your niche.

The algorithm is on your side.

1. Van der Blom, Richard. Content & Algorithm Playbook. 2026.
   https://sales.richardvanderblom.com/content-algorithm-playbook

2. Roth, Dan. "New Rules of Career Growth with
   LinkedIn's Dan Roth." YouTube, February 26, 2026.
   https://www.youtube.com/watch?v=oBXYER49TPM&t=251s

Conclusion

It is my sincere hope that this book gives you a solid foundation to show up on LinkedIn with more confidence, more strategy, and more results.

Whether you were unsure where to start, posting consistently and getting nowhere, watching people with half your experience outpace you, or just had a gut feeling you were playing the wrong game, this book was written for you.

But now you know the secret.

The comment section is where authority gets built, relationships start, and opportunity shows up.

You now have a system. You have the AICE framework. You know the daily routine. You know how to find the right conversations, show up with something worth saying, and build the kind of visibility that compounds over time.

You don't need more followers. You don't need to go viral. You don't even need to post every day or game the algorithm.

You just need to show up consistently, in the right places, with something real to say.

Additionally, The world is changing fast. AI is reshaping how people discover experts, how businesses get recommended, and how authority gets assigned.

The professionals who show up consistently, contribute genuinely, and build real relationships in their niche, they're the ones AI will surface, recommend, and validate.

You're not just building visibility for the people scrolling LinkedIn today. You're building the digital footprint that makes you discoverable tomorrow.

That's Comment Currency.

Now go leave a comment worth remembering.